How to Advocate Successfully for Your Child:

What *Every* Parent Should Know About Special Education Law

BY: GREER M. GURLAND, ESQ.

Why I Wrote This Book

Let me introduce myself. My name is Greer Gurland. I'm a mom of five kids with special needs. I am also a lawyer. I went to Harvard College and Harvard Law School. Then, I practiced corporate law and litigation in Manhattan before I stopped working and started raising my children with my husband. What I found, over the last decade, was that I used my advocacy skills very much in working with the schools to help my children receive the education that they needed.

And now, I work as a private advocate helping parents, and helping to teach other parents, how they can be the best advocate for their own children. I've been giving presentations, speaking to parents about how they can help their children, about all that they can do. And I wanted to share with you the substance of a presentation that I gave recently, because parents found it helpful and I was hoping that it might help you.

Let me also say that today there are more resources than ever for parents. If you know what you are looking for, Google and Yahoo can give you answers in seconds, if not guidance that can help a great deal. But what I have found, after counseling parents for years, is that parents do not know the very questions they should be asking about their children's education.

Just to be clear, I mean wonderful, well-meaning, devoted parents who would do anything for their kiddos--if only they knew what to do. In other words, me a decade ago, and still me, to a degree. Children change all the time. But in short, the point of this book is to help you know the questions you should be asking. That is more than half the battle.

Let me share with you the essentials of the law and strategies I have gleaned from my experience, personally as a mom of kiddos with special needs, and professionally, as a special education attorney. I promise to avoid the legal mumbo jumbo. You really don't need it.

In doing so, it is my sincere hope that you will know what questions to ask, when and how, and be able to advocate even more effectively for the child you love.

For my husband, Ira.

Table of Contents

Acknowledgements

This section is so important to me. I cannot express what a difference the following individuals have made in the lives of my children, and in my own life:

Thank you to clinical psychologist Elio Arrechea for his insight and intuitiveness, coupled with compassion. He has given my children amazing tools for living, and made me a better parent.

Thank you to Jayne Wesler and Staci Greenwald, special education attorneys at Sussan, Greenwald & Wesler. I am honored to call them colleagues and friends. I am grateful for their willingness to share their wisdom, and to take a chance on me.

Thank you to neuropsychologist Jill Brooks for understanding each child as an individual, and for playing such an active part in coming up with, and implementing, solutions.

Thank you to clinical psychologist and behaviorist Joanmarie Sackles for going above and beyond, and making a difference.

Thank you to elementary school teacher Ms. Eva Morton-Bell for suggesting to me, years ago, that I could help other parents, too.

Thank you to my children for teaching me more than I thought there was to know about myself.

Trust me, the list goes on.

A Special Thank You

A special note of gratitude to Children's Specialized Hospital, located throughout New Jersey, for their patient-centered approach, their responsiveness to the families they serve, and for their commitment to addressing the needs of children from diverse communities.

The Spanish edition of this book was made possible due to a generous contribution from Children's Specialized Hospital.

Introduction

I prefer to speak face-to-face, so even though you are reading my words today, please imagine that you are sitting comfortably at a presentation I am giving to parents, and that I am speaking directly to you.

You know, it's been very strange for me, getting ready to speak today. I usually prepare—a lot—for anything I do. But this was hard. And I couldn't figure out why. But, finally, I realized, it's because it's personal. But, once I get started, speaking to other parents like me, with kids with special needs, I could go on and on. I think it helps me to make sense of my own experience, to pass it along, and it makes me feel less alone.

I was speaking to one mom recently, my friend Valerie. She has a son with autism, like I do. And she said something that made me feel so good. She said that she loves speaking to other parents of kids with special needs because we know how to live.

She's right. We get to see what matters. We know that life is full of successes and failures. We know that it is a marathon and not a sprint. And we know that what makes our children special is not their special need. What makes our children special is what makes every child special: their unique personality and perspective—the perspective that they give to us.

At this point, when I am presenting, I usually jump up to show off the sculptures that my Russell has made for years from aluminum foil in my kitchen junk drawer. My son will take the aluminum foil from my junk drawer and make the most amazing sculptures. Works of art. I find them all over the house. And I thought it was just tin foil.

And, when we are driving in the car, he will regularly ask me a question that makes me stop and say, "I never thought of it that way." Our kids are creative kids who will do great things.

The challenges are just what I have to work through so the world can see them the way I do.

One of those challenges is advocating in school to get my children the education that they need. I am just like you: I want what is best for my children. What's tough for me is that I don't always know what that is. Like you, I would do anything for my children. But what's hard for me is that I don't always know what I should do.

And I realize that it's not just me. It is tough for us parents for some very real reasons.

It is so emotional—these are our children. I have had to learn to ignore a lot of judgment from other people to ask the questions I needed to, to get help. My son wouldn't put a spoon in his mouth at age four months—he wouldn't eat any solid food. I felt like I was the only one in the world in that situation.

It took me until my son was eighteen months, for me to reach out, to realize I could do more for him if I shared what was going on. And I took him to my local Children's Hospital for a feeding evaluation. That became a great start for him.

10

And a few weeks ago, I spoke with a woman, Rosana—a great mom, a great person. She is so upset. She is concerned that her daughter will never learn to read. She worries that the other second graders won't play with her daughter if they find out that her daughter leaves the room for extra help. And she worries about what her daughter will think of *herself* if she knows she has a disability.

I had those same worries. They are draining. It is hard to do the work of advocating for your children at the same time you're feeling all that. And I told Rosana what I'm sharing with you.

So, advocating for our children is hard because it is emotional. It is also hard because there is so much to know that is not intuitive—about your rights, the resources available, and how to go about accessing them.

And now that you've gotten me started, I could go on for hours. But I won't. I'm limiting myself to five lessons that I've learned, and that I remind myself of each day as I advocate for my children. And I hope you'll have lessons to share with me.

I lot of what I've learned has to do with the process. Bear with me for a cooking analogy; I love to cook. My mom's brisket recipe—I can smell it now—is so good, not because of the ingredients—you can guess the main one. It's great because of the method. You take that same aluminum foil that my son makes sculptures out of, and you crimp it tightly all around the edges of the pan. Then, you put it in the oven, and you leave it that way--for five-and-a-half, six hours. It's about the process.

And negotiating with the school, there's a method to that, too. Once I became more comfortable with that process, it became so much easier for me to change up the ingredients and deal with issues as they came along.

So, these are my lessons, about that process.

Lesson One—Know You Are Your Child's Best Advocate

You need to know—in your gut—that you are your child's best advocate, and that your child needs you. You have to know that you are up to this challenge, and that you have what it takes to get your child the education that he needs.

I remember an example from my working days, before I had children. The partner at the law firm called all of us young associates into the room to admonish us, to tell us that we were not to delegate any portion of our work. We were to be personally responsible for every word.

And his reason stuck with me. He said: "No one cares about your work the way you do." That *is* what it takes to make a meaningful difference. And, advocating for my children *is* my work now: Getting them what they need.

I also remember what a speech pathologist told me once, in the hallways of my son's preschool. She had to whisper it; but I can shout it. She said: "Parents don't know their power."

She's right. We parents have a unique perspective at that IEP table. We can ask any question, free from political pressure and budget issues. **You have the most power at that table when it comes to ensuring that your child gets the education that he needs.**

You also have a unique perspective on your child—vital information that the school needs to hear. For example, when my daughter breaks the Lego sculpture that my son made—my son who makes those foil sculptures—so you can imagine how much they mean to him—and he gets upset at her, and then she gets upset, I can tell you that she is going to do very badly on her math test that day. Not because she can't do the work, but because she will have trouble getting past that, emotionally. She will shut down.

And, as the parent, I can ask for a new test, as a start, so that the teacher can show that she has taught my daughter, and my daughter can demonstrate that she can learn. But, I can also ask for the school behaviorist to go in, to work with the teacher and my daughter, and to help figure out why she shuts down and how to help her in those times when she is having trouble getting past how she feels. That has been highly successful.

And when I am at home, and I see my son who has autism playing Legos with his sister, interacting socially, I can video tape that and share it with the school. And when I see him problem-solving, saying to my older son, "Take this"—meaning a certain toy, so that he can keep the one he really wants to play with, I can tell the school what I see. I can work with the school team to change the school environment to give him a chance to develop the potential I see. This is what we are doing. As a team, we decided to bring my son into another classroom that is less restrictive, little by little, to give him different opportunities to develop. Without my input, the school might not have seen the need.

So, that type of change—it doesn't always come about unless the parent speaks up about what she sees, and asks to be part of coming up with a solution.

So, be brave. Find a source of strength in you to be that confident mom or dad at the table, unafraid to ask a question or ask for help.

A school psychologist once told me, as we were standing outside the school building following one of those meetings: "Addressing your child's challenges does not take away from his strengths. That helped me a lot.

As a parent, think about how you got things done and what made you successful before you had children. Think about how you dealt with people, and tough situations. All of that will help you be your child's best advocate.

Notes

Notes

Lesson Two—Build The Relationship

I need to create a good working relationship with the school. I remind myself of a lesson from a negotiation class I took in law school, years ago. The professor, the famous Roger Fisher who wrote *Getting to Yes*, divided us up into groups of two. Each group had goals to negotiate for. And some teams played fair, and others did not play as fair.

At the end of the negotiation, the professor's surprise was that this was just round one. We had to go on to rounds two, three and four with the very same groups. At the very end, the teams that mutually got more of what they sought were the teams that played fair from the start.

So, I play fair. **Working with the school *is* a negotiation. And I have a long term goal: getting my children the education that they need.** I need the school's help today; but, I may need it even more so tomorrow. Today, I may be asking the school to increase my daughter's occupational therapy from two to three times per week, but next month I may be asking for an iPad (don't tell the principal!).

So, I take care of that relationship. It is so much easier to take care of it than to try to mend it afterwards. So how do I do that? I never make personal attacks. Even if I strenuously disagree with the significance of the data that the behaviorist has collected about my son, I never make it personal. No nasty emails, ever. If you need to write one to vent, go ahead. I have. Just don't hit "Send." Doing so won't help you reach your long term goal.

I also pick and choose my battles. I accept that I will lose some. I lose gracefully. I use it as an opportunity to build good will.

And I never blame. I tell my kids: "If you blame me because your shoes are lost, it doesn't really make me feel like helping you look for them." And I *want* the school to want to help my children. *I* don't want to make that hard for them.

I send "thank you" notes. If someone goes out of their way to help my child—for example, if my child is crying on the playground, and a paraprofessional helps ease her into the day—I send her a "thank you" note. And, I send a copy to her boss. (See the Appendix for a sample "thank you" note.)

I give credit to everyone else. And I show respect for the team by being open to all their ideas. I want them to hear mine. They have. When it came time to pick a new placement for my daughter, the school team preferred a more restrictive environment. I thought a less restrictive placement was appropriate, in light of what I was seeing her do socially, her needs socially, and how she responded to her peers.

And even though the team really disagreed with me, because we had a good long term working relationship, I think they believed me when I said that I would be open to seeing what the data showed, no matter which option we chose. And in that instance, when I cared deeply about the choice, they were willing to try it my way. And it turned out to be a great success. And I credit the team for being open to listening to me and working with me.

(On other occasions, I have chosen to "try it their way." In those instances, I have asked the team to take clear data going forward, so that we can all take a look at what about that choice has worked and what has not worked.)

I do what I say. If I say, "I agree with the IEP. I am going to sign it" then I sign it and walk it over to the Board of Education that day. I don't want to keep them guessing. And I don't lie. I check my facts. Because I want the team to believe me, to trust what I report.

So, in these ways, I play fair. I am nice. **But "nice" does not mean powerless.** My actions will convey that I will pursue what is in my child's best interests. If we can only take a small step today, great. I'll take that small step, and then come back tomorrow to see what next step we can take together.

And, although I do not enjoy confrontation, I will be confident when I am asking for what my child needs. I stay calm at meetings, because I want the team to understand that I am not asking out of emotion. I hope my love for my children is clear, but I am asking based on the data, the facts, and I have copies of reports to share with everyone—to make it easy.

I want the school to see that I know my rights. I don't have all the answers, but if something sounds funny to me during a meeting I will ask—at the meeting, and afterwards. And I don't give up. When the issue is important, like my daughter's placement, and the answer is "no," I take that as a starting point. And then I ask what would make it easier for the team to say "yes," and then, how we can get there.

And I do all that, by being prepared...

Notes

Notes

Lesson Three—Prepare

I need to prepare, which includes being organized.

A quick story:

When my son had a new case manager—the old one left the district—we had our first progress meeting. It was an eight-week progress meeting. We sat down in the principal's office. It was the case managers, the teachers, the therapists, the principal and myself. And the case manager started by saying: "Okay, Mrs. Gurland. This is how we will proceed. We'll hear from the teachers and then the therapists about what they see in your child..."

The principal interrupted her.
He said: "Oh, no. You don't know Mrs. Gurland!" (I still laugh.). The principal stopped the case manager because he knows that I come with my own list of concerns. I have a list that I write out. And I didn't invent this—I believe Pete Wright did, but it works great. It says:

What Mom Wants	School's Response	Resolved?

Here is an example of how my list might look, when I've filled it out to attend a meeting: (Also see the Appendix for another sample, and a blank form for you to copy.)

What Mom Wants	School's Response	Resolved?
Speech increased to three times per week. Ask classroom teacher to share math word problems with speech therapist so therapist can review math vocabulary		
Speech therapist to go into classroom, lunch and recess to observe language pragmatics.		
Add lunch bunch to facilitate social skills and interactions during lunch.		
Do occupational therapy evaluation with sensory component.		
Add Homework Club three days a week.		

The principal—even though we've disagreed at times—has been terrific. But he knows that if we don't get to the items on my list, I'll be back.

So, having that list, being prepared, makes a big difference. But, how do I come up with a list like that? I'm not an expert in speech and language pragmatics. The way is to have a terrific team of advisors. And, if you've been going to your local Children's Hospital, as I have, or seeing doctors, learning consultants in your community, you already have people on your team of advisors. They are so important.

Your team of advisors are the psychologists, the pediatric neurologists, the developmental pediatricians, the learning consultants, the occupational therapists, the physical therapists, the speech therapists, the nutritionists, the behaviorists—all those people who help you understand your child's needs and document them in their reports that you bring with you to the school meetings, to make the case for what your child needs.

In preparing, I make use of another negotiation lesson from that law school class: You win not by arguments—even good ones—but by the data. And in our case, the data can also include your own reports—of how often you see your child having a tantrum, or a videotape of your child showing how he behaves.

But, for me, the private evaluations from the doctors and therapists who have worked with my children have been crucial in showing the school what my children's needs are. I find that private evaluations can often be much more thorough than what the school can provide.

For example, my son—the one who makes those amazing tin foil sculptures, and has those great ideas when we are driving in the car—he has trouble writing. But, it's a shame for him not to be able to share those creative ideas. For years, I had spoken with the school about doing an assistive technologies evaluation. I wanted to see if we could bring in some type of computer device, or word prediction software, to help my son have a way of writing more quickly.

Finally, the school agreed to do an assistive technologies evaluation. I was thrilled. But, the person who happened to meet with my son that day did not see evidence that my son was ready. And all my saying that he was in fact ready, was not going to make a difference.

What did make a difference was taking my son to my local Children's Hospital and getting a private assistive technologies evaluation. That evaluator was able to match my son with technology that she thought he could use and that he was ready for. She chose a laptop and word prediction software (which, if you type the letter "t" it gives you choices such as "this" "that" and "the," so you can simply touch the screen to choose your word).

Next, I took that report to a local learning consultant. The learning consultant worked with my son using that technology. And I videotaped it. Then, I took that videotape and the reports from those two professionals and I brought them back to the school.

With that new data, the school was willing to reconsider and perform a new assistive technologies evaluation of their own. And, with all that new data, the school did agree to provide my son with a laptop—now an iPad—and word prediction software.

That technology has been a great success, helping my son not only have a means of written communication, but also greatly improving his confidence and independence. **And I credit the team for being open to all the data that I brought to them.**

So, in my case, those private evaluations have been crucial in helping the school understand what my child's needs are. And a team of advisors is so important in helping you to understand and present those needs to the school.

My team of advisors is so important to me that I have them written down on a slip of paper that I keep tacked on the bulletin board in my kitchen, so if I should get hit by a bus on the way home from the supermarket, my husband knows who to call. They are that important.

Being prepared may also include explaining your child's diagnosis to the school team. My son has a central auditory processing disorder. I would not expect every teacher to be familiar with that disorder or with how it would show up in my son.

But, if I can explain to the teacher that it may look like my son is willfully ignoring you, when you ask him to open a book or to put a pencil down, but that, in fact, he has not processed—understood—what you said to him, that can go a long way in helping my son have a better experience, and helping the teacher teach my son. I can share what has worked with me at home to insure my son's understanding, and what has worked in school in the past.

Being prepared also means knowing your rights. And I think—hands down—that knowing your rights is the most daunting. It was for me. But I can tell you exactly how to do it. This book is the perfect start. **In *this presentation, and with the additions for this book, I attempt to share the most important rights parents need to know, in order to be amazing advocates, in language we can all understand.***

There is always more to learn. There are other books, such as: Wrightslaw's: *From Emotions to Advocacy* by Pete Wright and Pam Wright. You can get it on Amazon. And, in New Jersey, the Education Law Center has *The Right to Special Education: A Guide for Advocates.* "Advocates" are people like you and me. The guide is a free document that you can download. If you live outside of New Jersey, the Education Law Center in your state likely has a similar publication.

But, the law is only part of it. Truly the parent perspective is essential. Go to panels given to parents in your community--like the one that I am re-creating in this book. From the other parents, you can learn strategies that have been helpful to them. You will learn **information that you can only get from other parents.**

In addition, every public district is required by law to have a local parent special education committee. And, in my district, they meet every month in the library of one of our middle schools. You can go to your local Office of Special Services, or any local public school, and ask for the contact information, so that you can be invited to those meetings. And there you will hear presentations, and speak with parents who can share ideas that have worked for other students in your community. Then, you'll have more ideas that you can bring to the table when you have meetings about your children.

Put your name of the email list when you go to those meetings. You'll very likely get emails telling you about local advocacy training programs for parents. I found out about one in my community at my local Children's Hospital that was geared to parents of children with autism, but really, the advocacy information would be helpful to parents of children with varying special needs. So, go to any programs that you see that are like that. And I continue to go to them, because there is always something new to learn.

But, today, I would like to share enough specifics of the law, so that if you are thinking, "Well, maybe it is time for me to think about special education services for my child," then you know exactly what to do, now. **And what I am going to share is basically the same in every district in New Jersey. Moreover, it's pretty much the same all over the country with very little variation.**

Your Legal Rights

Let's get started. Your local public school district may provide services to your child on the day your child turns three, if he qualifies. My kids walked into their preschool program with their birthday cupcakes on their third birthday. But what that means, for you as a parent, is that six months before then, **when your child is two-and-a-half years old, you need to write a letter to the Director of the Office of Special Services.**

How do you get his or her name and address? You can go online to the homepage for your school district and look under Offices/Special Services. Or, you can just walk into any local public elementary school, middle school, or high school. Go to the main office. Ask the secretary for the name, number and address of the Director of the Office of Special Services. They all know who that is.

Then, write a letter—and don't hesitate because you don't have a special form, even though there are many forms available, or you don't know what to say. Simply write:

"Dear Director,

I am very concerned about my daughter, Jill. Please evaluate her for special education at your earliest convenience. I am very grateful for your help.

Sincerely,

_____ "

(I include another sample, showing letter form, in the Appendix to this book.)

Sign the letter, date it, and walk it over to the secretary of the Director. Introduce yourself. The secretary can sign and date your letter if you ask. Keep a copy of the letter. Hold on to that letter because it starts a time clock. **By law, the school only has a certain number of days (most likely twenty calendar days) to get back to you and to start the process of evaluating your child.**

If your child takes part in Early Intervention, which is the Federal program for children ages zero to three, Early

Intervention providers can help you send that letter. They can also go with you to the first meeting you will then have with the school district.

After you send your letter, you will hear from the school. Usually you will hear from a case manager, who will be your main contact with the school's special education team. The case manager will schedule a first meeting with you to discuss your concerns.

When you go to that first meeting, *bring all your data from your terrific team of advisors*. Bring those reports. The school will look at them and speak to you about your concerns. Together, you and the school will determine what additional evaluations the school needs to do, to see if your child qualifies for special education and related services.

So how does your child qualify? *A child qualifies, and services are provided, when a child has a disability that adversely affects the educational performance of the child.* **The child does not have to be failing. And educational performance is not just academics. Emotional, behavioral, social challenges—they all matter, and are all aspects of a child's functioning in school that are appropriate for the school to consider.** They all matter because they all are important in accomplishing the purpose of special education. That purpose is *to educate students with disabilities so they are prepared for post-secondary education, employment, and independent living.*

That mom Rosana whom I told you about--her child had to pick two words to describe herself, and one of them she picked was "stupid." That matters. That is a reason for a school to look at what it is doing for a child. But the school needs you to tell them that. That is part of that vital information, vital perspective, that you have. And even better if you can get those words on tape.

In evaluating your child, the school follows an *"academic,"* versus a *"medical"* model. What that means is that **you as the parent need to be explaining to the school district how your child's disability affects his ability to perform in school.**

For instance, one of my sons had feeding issues. At first, the school viewed that as a medical issue. But, with a report from the nutritionist at my local Children's Hospital, I was able to document and explain to them how my child's being able to maintain his nutrition during the day was essential for him to attend, focus and learn.

With that information, the school was willing to provide home food therapy, and also a paraprofessional in school to assist my child at lunch. My son received this service, in preschool and in elementary school.

When you meet with the school, it does help to know the buzz words. ***Your child is entitled to an "appropriate" education. And, that does not mean the best education, or one that helps your child reach his potential—even though that's what every parent wants, of course.*** An "appropriate" education means one that enables your child to make meaningful gains. So, when I am speaking with the school, I always speak to that standard. I say, ***"My child need this..,"*** ***"My child needs that..."***

Also, your child is entitled to be educated in the *"least restrictive environment."* That means close to your home, and to the extent possible, with his typical, non-disabled peers. The least restrictive setting has to be one in which your child makes progress, and does not regress, or stagnate.

If the team evaluates your child, and determines that your child is eligible, the team will meet with you again to design an **"Individualized Education Program"** or **"IEP"** for your child. The IEP states your child's program and services (among other important items such as your child's current levels of achievement, and goals for your child for the year). The school can also provide services through something called a **504 Plan**. (See the Crucial Question section of this book for a discussion of the important differences.)

The IEP should grow out of your child's needs. It should not be based on what your school happens to have in place. Know that a school district generally does have many options — various programs and placements—to meet children's varying needs. (I know, because my children have been in all of them!) It's called a "continuum of services"— which really just means there's an array of options. It helps you to know that going in. If the school team offers only one option, specifically ask what other programs the team considered.

The Placement Options That May Be Available For Your Child

The school has *"out-of-district placements"* (which would be on the more restrictive end). When people talk about out-of-district placements, they usually mean private schools that educate children who have a certain need. The schools are considered private, but if the school sends your child, the school pays the tuition. The law entitles your child to a free education.

And then there are many programs that are *in-district*, meaning they are housed in your local school district:

For example, *"self-contained programs"* are in-district programs that consist of special education classrooms where the teacher is a special education teacher and the students have special education needs.

There are what are called "***inclusion classes***." These are classes where there are mainstream children and special education students taught side by side by a general education teacher (or "gen ed" teacher) and a special education teacher.

There are placements where the child is in the mainstream classroom for most of the day, but is pulled out of the classroom and goes to a separate room, sometimes called a "***resource room***," often for language arts, or math. In this resource room, the child is taught by a special education teacher in a much smaller environment (often four to eight students). (See the Appendix for more information about potential placements, from most to least restrictive.)

That's the placement. Then, there are also services that may be appropriate for your child—and there are a good number. (Technically, they are called "**related services**"). They include **occupational therapy, physical therapy, and speech therapy** that can be provided in school.

Your child's IEP may contain other supports:

There are **paraprofessionals** who can assist children in school. There are **assistive technologies**, like the iPad my son uses, and hearing devices to help children with auditory processing disorders, for example.

The school can also provide the support of a **behaviorist**, if warranted. There is a school psychologist who can be brought into your child's school program.

Services that the school provides to your child can include an **Extended School Year** program ("ESY"). This usually consists of a six- to eight- week program that the school provides during the summer.

Your child's IEP program can also include many, many **modifications** to school curriculums, homework assignments and testing accommodations, to meet the "needs"—not wants—

33

of children with special needs. *(See the Appendix for a listing of many frequently used modifications that might apply to your child.)*

Discuss placement and program options with your terrific team of advisors. Get their input. A letter from a physician who is familiar may recommend a program for your child. Ask for his or her professional opinion in writing, as part of their report, so that you can share this data with the school team for them to consider.

The IEP document, the document that you and the team will come up with that describes the program and services for your child for the year, also sets goals for one year. The goals need to be measurable. They need to be written in a way that lets you look at them a year from now and be able to tell if they have been achieved.

By law, the school needs to meet with you to review your child's IEP each year, but **the IEP document can change whenever it needs to**. And, you don't have to have just one IEP meeting per year. In fact, with my own elementary school students, I have progress meetings with the school every eight weeks. I request them.

I find that at those meetings, where you have the case manager, the teachers and the therapists all sitting down discussing your child—what they see, and the problems and solutions they've tried—you get those creative solutions. These strategies often cost the school no money but can really make a big difference in how your child functions. And kids change fast. A lot goes on in a child's life. I find it so much more helpful to talk about the child as a team more than once a year.

Each time you meet with the school and get a new proposed IEP document—and often, the case manager will hand you one at the meeting—**don't sign the IEP at the meeting.** Take it home and sleep on it. Just sign the attendance sheet; that's what I do. Take the document home, and give yourself time to process it. Consult a spouse, a friend—or someone from your terrific team of advisors. Make sure that you are comfortable with it.

And, I have to say, I am lucky. My kids are receiving amazing services and a wonderful education. And that has been through working with the school. But, I know that should negotiation ever fail, dispute resolution procedures are available —"**mediation**" and "**due process hearings.**" However, in the majority of cases, with negotiation you can advocate for your child and do a tremendous amount to ensure they get a terrific education. *(For more information about dispute resolution procedures including mediation, and a sample mediation request, see Crucial Questions and the Appendix.)*

Notes

Notes

Lesson Four—Follow Through

Once you have an IEP—once I have an IEP, I have to make sure that it's implemented.

A quick story: My elementary school son was talking to me about his day, and from what he was saying I had a question as to whether the paraprofessional that's designated in his IEP was there for the times that she was supposed to be.

What did I do? I asked to meet with the teacher. I sat with her at a little table in her classroom, and I asked her to write down for me the days and the times that the para was in the classroom. And when we did that, it became clear that the facts did not match up with what the IEP called for.

As soon as that information became clear, the principal corrected the problem. I credited the school for taking action. **But, for that to happen, I needed to be a presence.**

The school needs to see that you care. It makes a big difference for you to be involved. I try to get in to that school whenever I can—whether it's reading a story, dropping off a violin that one of my kids forgot, or delivering chicken nuggets to the cafeteria. It's helpful to be available. You hear what is going on and can have those informative side chats with teachers and other staff. You are able to build that all-important relationship with the school, and let the school know that you realize that what they do every day matters.

When each new year begins, I make a point of communicating with each new teacher. I send an email to the teachers with a little description of my child and I invite communication--about matters big and small, positive and negative. And, when I do hear about a problem, first, I offer support. Then, I ask what's been done, what happened, and what we can try next.

I make sure to spend time to communicate informally with teachers individually, face to face, outside of the larger meetings. I protect their confidence.

When I have any significant, formal communication with the school, I always keep a record of it. (See the Appendix for the "Communication Log" form I use to keep a quick record of these conversations.)

After you fill in your chart with your notes from your IEP meeting, make a copy of it and send it to the team, along with my thank you note. You want to make sure that everything that happens that is significant is in writing.

Any agreement that you make with a teacher, with the case manager, with the school—always make sure that you document it. Recollections differ.

The Child Binder

Your child will bring home so many reports and pieces of important information. I keep it all together by placing everything in one three-ring binder, one for each child. That way, I keep my notes, records, examples of my child's work, and all evaluations in one place. I place the current IEP on top. I bought an electric three-hole punch which makes life easy for busy parents; I think it is the best thing since sliced bread.

Include in your binder all important documents in chronological order—I like to keep the most recent on top. *Keep this book you are reading in the front pocket, so the team will know you have informed yourself.* If you set up a binder, then you will be automatically prepared for your next meeting. (See the Appendix for more on how to set up your Child Binder.)

In addition, having such a binder creates a convenient record should there ever be a dispute down the road. If you ever meet with a mediator or a judge, that binder will be useful evidence of what happened, and what really is going on with your child.

Notes

Notes

Lesson Five—You Are Not Alone

Please know that you are not alone. And, *my child* asked me to add that **your child is not alone**.

I get overwhelmed. But, I remind myself that I am part of a powerful community. *We* are part of a powerful community. I regret that I didn't go to programs like the ones I speak at now sooner. So, you are way ahead of me in doing this research now.

And, I didn't know about special education parent meetings, but when I did, I felt funny identifying myself. I was embarrassed to walk into the room and be the mom whom everyone will know is the mom who has a child with a special need. I know it's hard to walk in that room. But just do it. Please. You will see that there are so many people who share your struggle and want to help.

Valerie, my friend I told you about, whose son has autism, he's in college now. My oldest is thirteen; but I see already that I wasted a lot of time worrying. I still will. I think that's part of having children, in general.

But, my children have also given me so much—helped me to see how I want to live. **When I work to show the world what is so special about my kids, it reminds me to look for what is special in *everyone* in my life, including me.**

Take time for yourself. I write poetry and personal essays that grow out of my experiences; you will create your own amazing stories. But, being parents is an emotional journey we share.

You are great parents. *It is how invested you are emotionally that makes you your child's best advocate.*

And, communicating with parents like you helps me be stronger—in addition to making me cry. So, thank you.

Crucial Questions—Please Read

Parents have asked me the questions I share on the following pages, numerous times—for good reason: the answers matter. Let me give you my best advice as to these crucial questions.

What about the stigma?

Parents worry about this a lot. I am one of them.

But I got over it when I realized that not dealing with my child's issues was not making them invisible. **Everyone sees when a child is struggling.** *And the child feels it.* I realized, in time—I am only human—that I could do far more for my children by getting them classified and taking advantage of the amazing special education laws we have in this country.

Plus, don't be scared if you had a bad experience in special education as a child. The landscape has changed. **It is a new world of teaching, of understanding about learning differences.** And we know that early intervention can make a big difference.

In private practice, I have seen that when underlying learning issues are not addressed, children can go on to develop anxiety, depression or other emotional issues that are tied to the frustration of having a learning difference.

In other words, you can worry about the stigma—I did—but still do what you need to in order to get your child the services he or she needs. *You will be making your child stronger and enabling him to feel better about himself, ultimately.*

What is the difference between an IEP (Individualized Education Program) and a 504 Plan?

They are both documents that a school can use to set forth special services for children who have special needs. They can accomplish the same goals, but they are not exactly alike. If the choice is up to me, I usually opt for an IEP. I just find that they come with more procedural safeguards, and parents and other attorneys have told me that schools follow them more faithfully in their experience. You could say there tends to be more accountability with an IEP. Of course, some school districts have better track records than others.

The 504 Plan

In terms of what they are, a 504 Plan is a document that exists by virtue of the federal Americans with Disabilities Act. It applies in school, but it does not only apply to schools. It entitles all individuals with disabilities to **"equal access."**

In the school setting, this means access to an education like a non-disabled student. Technically, in order to qualify for a 504 Plan a child must first have a disability. That means that the child **"has a mental or physical impairment that substantially limits one or more major life activity."**

I find that school districts themselves are sometimes unaware that this "major life activity" does not have to be your child's ability to get good grades. It may be his or her ability to focus, or ability to stay emotionally regulated in school.

A 504 Plan can be written to include just about anything that a school could put into an IEP. But, more often 504 Plans are used to address medical conditions. A student with a visual impairment might have a 504 Plan that provides for readings in Braille.

The IEP

An IEP falls under "The Individuals with Disabilities Education Act" ("IDEA")—a Federal statute that is about ensuring a **"free, appropriate public education"** for students with disabilities.

It is often said that an IEP is the appropriate document when special education is necessary (meaning teaching by a teacher with special education training), and not just modifications or accommodations, like extended time or assistive technology.

To quality for an Individualized Education Program ("IEP"), a student: 1) must have a disability, 2) which affects his or her academic performance, such that 3) the student is in need of special education and related services.

Remember, "education" is a broad concept. It includes not only academics, but behavior, emotional and social functioning—as well as activities of daily living, including toileting.

***

To me, an IEP is often worth fighting for. The big difference is the protection that goes along with each one.

Some attorneys I know describe a 504 Plan as a "handshake," and an IEP as a "contract"—which it is. This fact is also why it is important for you to read your IEP carefully. The school will be required by law to follow the IEP terms—and only it's terms. (Unless of course you choose to deny services, which it is your right to do.)

As a parent and an attorney, it bothers me that the 504 team can change a 504 Plan, sometimes without notifying the parent. In contrast, an IEP cannot change unless the school follows specific procedures that include letting you know and giving you a chance to participate in the decision-making.

Other procedural safeguards that attend an IEP include the parental right to request a meeting to discuss your child's progress whenever you see the need. The school must respond within a certain time frame.

An IEP also gives you the right to mediation and due process, described further in this book. While you can file for mediation if you have a 504, most often I see IEP documents as the subject of mediation and due process hearings.

Another instance in which the protections of an IEP can help a child are in cases of **bullying**. There are, too frequently, instances in which children with disabilities are involved in cases of bullying, accused of being the bully. And children with 504 plans, or no plans, have been suspended for their actions.

But if a child has an IEP, and it's determined that the child's disability is in part the cause of the child's difficulties relating to his or her peers (in other words the "bullying" is in fact "a manifestation of the student's disability"), then a different approach has to be taken. The school may need to put a behavior modification plan in place to help the child deal with his emotions or address his behaviors, instead of punishing him for them.

So, when possible, when a child qualifies, an IEP can be preferable to a 504 Plan.

In New Jersey, it can be useful to know that in order to give an IEP the school team must select one of fourteen eligibility classifications. While the category does not determine what services your child will get, the categories give you a sense of the breadth of disabilities that the IEP is meant to encompass —no matter what state you live in.

49

The fourteen classifications for IEP eligibility in New Jersey are:

Auditorily Impaired

Autistic

Cognitively Impaired

Communication Impaired

Emotionally Disturbed

Multiply Disabled

Deaf/Blindness

Orthopedically Impaired

Other Health Impaired

Preschool Child with a Disability

Social Maladjustment

Specific Learning Disability

Traumatic Brain Injury

Visually Impaired

A few more thoughts about the choice between IEP and 504 Plan:

There is no right choice. The goal for you as the parent is getting your child the services he needs. If the school is succeeding in providing those services under a 504, great. If not, it generally makes sense to request an IEP if the facts substantiate your request. An IEP is, practically speaking, and in my legal experience, easier to enforce.

What about retaliation? My child with special needs has a younger sibling who is in the same school.

Retaliation is not what I have seen as the result of advocating respectfully for my children. And, professionally, what I more often find is that schools bend over backwards to ensure that they follow the rules with respect to all family members.

Also know that such retaliation—should it ever occur—would be an illegal abuse of power.

At my first meeting with the school, the child study team school offered to do a *social history*, a *psychological evaluation* and an *educational evaluation*. What else can I ask for?

The IEP team is required to assess your child in all areas of suspected disability. Remember, that includes emotional, behavioral concerns—as well as the ability to perform activities of daily living.

Schools will often add a **speech evaluation** if language is a concern. They will often readily add an **occupational therapy (OT) evaluation** to address handwriting. If your child has sensory issues, ask that the OT evaluation include a sensory component.

A PT or **physical therapy evaluation** may be necessary if the child's ability to maneuver safely and appropriately in school is an issue.

Certainly, schools have performed other evaluations, based on the disability suspected, including:

· **psychiatric evaluations,**
· **assistive technology evaluations,**
· **feeding evaluations,**
· **functional behavioral assessment**
(for use in formulating behavior intervention plans to address numerous possible issues in school).

When in doubt, ask what evaluation would help the team get a better understanding of your child's issues relating to X. Suggest options that seem relevant to you.

If the team conducts evaluations and comes back with findings that you do not believe capture your child's strengths and needs, you can request further evaluations by the school team, or an independent evaluation. See "When Should I Request an Independent Evaluation?" in this section.

How Do I Read These School Evaluations?

You don't need to be a learning consultant in order to make use of those school evaluations and advocate effectively. You just need to know a few basics, and the right questions to ask.

The school generally administers two tests to your child when considering eligibility for an IEP or Individualized Education Program:

1) A **Psychological Evaluation**
2) An **Educational Evaluation**

The Psychological Evaluation is a measure of your child's cognitive **potential,** measured using an IQ (intelligence quotient) test in most cases. Most schools use the WISC or Wechsler Intelligence Scale for Children. As discussed elsewhere in this book, there are other IQ tests that may be appropriate to get an accurate assessment of your child's potential, and get around the effect of the disability in order to test the child's potential.

The Educational Evaluation is a measure of **achievement**. It is supposed to show how much your child has learned. I have most often seen schools use the WJ or Woodcock-Johnson Test of Achievement.

The law requires that the school sit down with you to review these two test reports and explain them to you. In my experience, you need to ask certain questions and let them know you are interested in taking a close look at them together.

You will be looking primarily at the numerical test scores that the school should report for each test. You need to know that for both tests—which contain subtests—the average score is 100.

As a parent, you are looking for consistent scores. If your child has an IQ of 100, then his or her achievement should be approximately the same. Certain tests may be higher or lower, and reveal strengths or weaknesses. **A child will likely be considered to be achieving commensurate with his or her potential when the IQ and achievement scores match up.**

This is why it is so crucial to get an accurate IQ—it sets the bar for what your child will be expected to learn. If your child's IQ is an underestimate, your child may be considered to be achieving commensurate with his or her potential when that is not in fact the case.

In other words, the law entitles your child to receive meaningful educational benefit from his program, meaning that he is making meaningful progress. But you can't know if your child is making meaningful gains if you don't know what your child is capable of achieving. You need the test scores for that.

When discrepancies in the scores exist, you need to ask what weakness they point out and how the team can address them. For example, a low math fluency score despite a high IQ in the math-related subtests may be a sign of a math learning disability. A high verbal IQ and low reading fluency may reflect a different learning disability—for instance, dyslexia.

Discrepancies *within* either the IQ test or the achievement testing may also be cause for concern. Don't just look at the average of the scores which is what the full scale IQ tells you.

For example, a full scale IQ on the WISC can look typical —a score of 100—but, in fact, disguise the fact that the child has significant strengths and weakness. A child may have a verbal comprehension score that is above average, and a perceptual reasoning score (correlated with math) that is much lower. That type of discrepancy might occur in a child with a math learning disability, sometimes called a non-verbal learning disability. As a parent, look for differences of more than 15 points between any of the subtests. Ask the school what they indicate and propose to address them.

Also know that if the achievement scores are higher than the IQ score, the IQ scores may be wrong—meaning your child's actual IQ is higher. (Special education lawyers put it this way: "A child rarely outperforms his own potential.")

Get full information for everyone's benefit. If the school does not convert the raw scores from the test data into standard scores where 100 is the mean, ask them to do so. I also ask the school to give me the data showing how much each subtest score deviates (in terms of standard deviations) from the mean. Many computer-generated school reports now report how far the score is from the norm, and flag for you any discrepancies that are outside a certain number of standard deviations from the norm.

Do let the team know you are looking at those scores, and want their help, in interpreting your child's strengths and weakness, and designing programming to address those findings. And save these score reports in your Child Binder for each year, so that you can easily make comparisons over time.

What if my relationship with the school is already fractured?

Begin to repair it now. It is possible. Arrange a meeting with the school team to talk about your relationship with the school. Admit where you misunderstood the school's intentions and ask to begin again, working cooperatively.

I'm afraid to go to mediation myself and I can't afford a lawyer. What do I do?

"Feel the fear and do it anyway."

That's a quote I keep in my kitchen.

If you can go to an IEP meeting, you can go to mediation. It's actually easier. You will most likely meet with a few representatives of the school in your local Board of Education, in a small conference room, with a mediator from the State.

The mediator will try to help you and the school reach agreement. He or she will ask you your concerns and how they might be resolved. She will ask the same of the school's representative—usually the Director of Special Services attends. If you bring an attorney, the school's attorney will attend as well. Often the case manager attends. **Feel free to bring a friend for support.**

Once the mediator hears from both sides, she will often separate the parties into two rooms. She will then act as the broker—going back and forth between you and the school, trying to see if she can bring about agreement on a solution.

If you and the school reach an agreement you can both live with, the mediator will place the agreement in writing. The agreement is binding.

If you fail to agree, the mediator will help you to convert your mediation request into what is called a "**due process petition.**" (Of course, it is your choice, whether or not to proceed.) In practical terms, this just means that you will be scheduled for another mediation—but this one will be called a settlement conference, and the "mediator" will be a judge. You will most likely meet in your local court house, in a conference room. Again, you can do this. It is just a meeting.

If the parties agree to a settlement, the judge makes it official. If not, a hearing date will be scheduled. At this hearing, the judge will hear evidence from you and the school. A court official will give you more information about how the hearing will proceed, and what you need to do to prepare.

Would I be better off just moving to another school district?

Parents have asked this often. The unfortunate answer is that it is not clear that will help. While some districts have better track records, and better special education funding and programs than others, these programs are highly personnel-dependent, and personnel changes frequently.

If you are in a district with clearly inadequate services, moving may help. But **in most cases, it is not a panacea.**

If you are planning a move, it does plan to do your research beforehand. Ask around, and learn what services the town you are considering has to offer. I would advise that you call a local special education attorney, and ask to run by them the names of the towns you have in mind. Most likely, he or she will tell you where to steer clear—again, noting that the landscape changes all the time.

What if I've done everything "right" and the school still won't help me?

That is the time to seek legal counsel or file for mediation on your own. See sample mediation form, completed, in the Appendix.

When I was a young parent, the word "Mediation" frightened me. But believe, me, you can do it. Doing so is actually simpler and quicker than I realized when I was starting out.

What do I do if, at a meeting, a team member says something that I know is not true?

Ask them to put it in writing. You can simply say, "If that is the District's position, please put it in writing for me." Or, "Are you saying X? If so, I will write down that that is your position and ask you to sign it for me."

If the case manager says that the law requires something that sounds fishy to you, ask her to send you the statute to which she refers. Repeat what she has told you in your "thank you" letter.

Should I record the meeting?

It depends. You most likely have the legal right to tape the meeting. Your jurisdiction likely requires that you provide advance notice to your case manager. This can be helpful later on, if you are pretty certain the IEP team is going to state a violation of your rights, or a position they will deny later.

However, it can seem confrontational. Unless the relationship is already soured, I usually suggest foregoing taping, and sending a confirmation thank you later, instead, to create a record. I just find that problem solving happens more freely when the parties do not have to worry about being recorded.

What do I bring to an IEP meeting?

The most important job for you as a parent at an IEP meeting is to listen for the district's position, remain cooperative and be open to hearing all options. But in terms of what to bring with you, I suggest the following:

1. Your **Child Binder**—see the Appendix for what to put in this.

2. Bring copies of **any new private evaluations** so that you will have enough copies for everyone on the team.

3. **Your Chart of Parent Requests**—see the Appendix for a form you can use. Remember, this is where you write down your concerns, and where you will note what the school says in response, to create your record.

4. **Paper and a pencil** to take notes, of course—remember this meeting is a negotiation and it pays to listen to the school's interests so you can try to come up with solutions that meet their interests, as well as yours.

5. Feel free to bring any individual who will provide **support**.

Also, make a note to yourself to remember to ask for another meeting in eight weeks (or however long you believe makes sense) to follow up on outstanding items and review your child's progress.

What do I do if I don't think the case manager captured my child in the IEP?

Every parent has a right to contribute to the IEP document their own parent input. I suggest crafting your own statement as to your child's needs and concerns. Email it to the case manager in a form that is easy to cut and paste directly into the IEP. Ask, in writing, that the case manager include your statement in the Present Levels of Academic Performance or in the Parent's Concerns. That is what I do.

If the case manager refuses, then ask the case manager to include your statement, and your request that it be included, in the section of the IEP entitled "Parent Requests Not Met."

What do I do if I disagree with the results of the district's testing?

Discuss with the team, first. The team may agree with you, or offer to collect more data. Or, this may be the time to ask for an independent evaluation. **One of a parent's most powerful rights is the right to request what is referred to as an "independent educational evaluation," or "IEE."**

An IEE is an evaluation of your child by someone other than the school staff. It is by a person you agree to, but at the district's expense. It gives you a chance to have someone who is more independent take a look at the issue. The district should give you names to choose from, and while there is often a cost limit, you have the right to approve the independent evaluator.

I suggest that you call the evaluators you are considering. Ask the potential evaluator if she is prepared to opine on the question in your mind—i.e., ask the evaluator if she will answer —meaning, give her professional opinion—as to whether your child has the language ability to be in a certain classroom at issue.

The right to request an independent evaluation is so powerful because a district cannot just say "no" to your request. In order to deny a parent the right to an independent evaluation, the school needs to file for mediation, basically to explain why it is denying your request. You should receive a copy. If the school fails to do this, file yourself.

The Importance of Proper Assessments and the Role of Independent Educational Evaluations

One important instance in which you might choose to request an independent evaluation is when you believe the assessment tool was not a good fit for your child, considering his or her challenges. We often say that those assessments **test the child's disability**.

For instance, there are numerous IQ tests. Most often, school districts administer the WISC. If your child is weak with verbal skills, as many children with autism are, this test may not reveal your child's full potential.

Say, the district conducts an evaluation using the WISC and reports a score of 67. You might look at the school's report, and say to yourself: "I know my child's IQ is higher, based on what I see." You would have the right to ask for an independent evaluation, and to ask that a different test be administered.

For children with autism, a TONI (or Test of Non-Verbal Intelligence) can sometimes better reveal their cognitive potential. Ask for the learning consultant on the IEP to help you pick an alternative assessment or request an independent evaluator with experience and the ability to pick a more suitable assessment. Ask questions.

The independent evaluator will provide a new assessment and report. The team is required to consider these new findings.

Should I waive my right to triennial evaluations?

By law, the district needs to re-evaluate your child every three years to be sure your child still qualifies for services. These evaluations are the "triennial evaluations" and usually consist of at least a psychological assessment (to measure IQ) and an education assessment (to assess academic achievement). Sometimes a case manager will say: "I think we all agree on your child's program, so—if you are in agreement—we don't need to do re-evaluations of your child." The law would otherwise require revaluations every three years.

Why you usually want to say "no" to waiving this updated testing:

In order to track your child's progress, you need to see the standardized testing over the years so that you can compare achievement scores and IQ scores. (See "How Do I Read These School Evaluations?") Are your child's achievement scores going up or down?

You can only do this if you gather the data. In general, I recommend that when the case manager asks, express appreciation for the offer to pass, but opt for the tests, as they can only enlighten the team as to your child's progress and any new areas of weakness to target.

Report card grades are not a good substitute for standardized testing; grades are just too subjective.

When to waive: Waive these evaluations if you are having private evaluations that would conflict, or if you are certain that your child's achievements are so great and his needs not otherwise apparent that there is a real concern about losing IEP eligibility.

Keep in might that eligibility is based on more than the test scores. If the teachers who work with your child recommend services, that matters. Also, social, emotional, behavioral and pragmatic issues all need to be considered—no matter how well your child scores on any test.

Plenty of children are considered "**twice exceptional**" or "**2E**." They have great cognitive ability but struggle in some areas due to one or more disabilities that affect their educational performance. (I have one of those special students myself.)

Of course, another reason to defer testing is if you do not have faith and confidence in the person who will administer the assessment. I might advise seeking a private evaluation in this case.

What Exactly is the Fifteen-Day Rule?

This one is important. Very important.

When you get your very first IEP for your child, it will only go into effect if you sign it. (And if you have concerns, you can sign it with an asterisk, or a note you write in next to your name, indicating that you are signing so that services can begin, but that you are not in complete agreement with the terms and reserve your rights)

After the very first IEP, every successive IEP will go into effect—whether or not you sign it—fifteen calendar days (including weekends) after you receive the "proposed IEP."

If you want to keep a new proposed IEP from going into effect, you need to file for mediation before these fifteen days run out.

It is not enough to tell the case manager that you disagree, or to tell the Director of Special Services that you will not sign. **To prevent the new proposed IEP from going into effect, y**ou *must file the mediation request per the instructions on the state website.* Doing so invokes what is referred to as "**stay put**." What "Stay put" means, in practical terms, is that the school cannot make whatever changes they put into the new IEP and must wait until the mediation request is heard and the matter is resolved.

When is it important to file for mediation and prevent that "proposed IEP" from going into effect? It is important to file when the proposed IEP contains a *change* in programming that you disagree with, or a *reduction or elimination* of services with which you take issue.

If you have only minor disagreements over terms of services or working of goals, you can email the case manager and attempt to work out these items without jumping to file. That is what I do, and so far I have never needed to file on my own behalf. But **if you do attempt to resolve these small matters —which I suggest you do—ask the case manager to write "Draft" on the IEP.**

"Draft" is not the same as "Proposed." If the IEP is a draft, the fifteen days do not start running. Make sure you have the "draft" copy in hand, or the case manager's agreement to call it a draft in writing.

You will get your own sense of your case manager's commitment to working with you to resolve any outstanding items. I find that most individuals who work in special education have a sincere desire to do the right thing and to help students succeed. I hope that you will have the largely positive experiences that I have had in my school district.

If I do want the school to make a few relatively minor changes to the IEP, how do I tell the case manager?

I usually send a letter by email, requesting those changes. I clearly set forth the specific changes I am requesting on each page. Keep a printed copy of your request, so that checking the revised IEP, when you get it, is simple.

Here is a sample of the kind of letter I write to request revisions to a proposed IEP. I usually email this type of letter, and print a copy for my records.

Dear [Case Manager],

Thank you so much for the proposed IEP and for the entire team's efforts to address Mike's needs. Please incorporate the revisions below to reflect our meeting discussion and address Mike's needs.

Kindly send me the revised IEP to review. I am grateful to the team for their involvement and thoughtfulness.

I am confident that we can reach agreement. Please confirm that this IEP will be considered a draft, and that the fifteen-day review period will not begin, until we can iron out these few matters.

Sincerely,
[parent]

Page 1: BIP: Change No to Yes as there is in fact such a behavior intervention plan in place.

Page 2: Behavior Therapy should be listed as once per week (not per month) as agreed to at IEP meeting.

Page 3: Please note that Mike's trial of Daytrana was not effective and has been discontinued.

Page 4: Behavioral Needs: Please include current behavior plan.

Page 5: Please revise "Auditory Needs" to reflect Mike's CAP diagnosis.

Visual Needs: Please reflect that Mike is color blind (red-green; blue/purple)

PLAAFP: Please send revised PLAAFP (Present Levels of Academic Achievement and Functional Performance) if there is one. The teachers' reports seem to be the ones from last year.

page 11: Please add to the MODIFICATIONS for All Subject Areas:

- Additional processing time
- Periodic check of long-term assignments with timelines
- Repeat-reword directions to ensure student understands the assignment
- Modify class and homework as needed
- Provide copies of notes
- Weekly communication via email by teachers at (insert parent email) of how student is doing
- Modify classwork and homework as needed due to student's slow pace; modify to show mastery
- Copy of textbooks for home
- Allow student to use modified agenda page; teachers to check off, daily, that student has correctly recorded homework, HW handed in, and no assignments missing

Parents' statement: Please add to the IEP the following parents' statement:

"Parent has provided executive skills tutoring one-on-one at private expense since Mike's last report card. At the April 4, 2016 meeting, parent asked for school to provide similar assistance in

school instead. Team advised parent that they would like to try BIP first, instead. Parents are following team recommendation. However, parents still believe OT/executive functioning training in school is appropriate and Mike himself has asked that this be provided."

My child is doing great—so says the school—but it's only because we do so much outside tutoring and give him so much homework help. What should we do?

Stop. It was so incredibly difficult for me to take this advice, but **unless you allow the school to see how their program is—or is not—working, it is hard, practically speaking, for the team to justify changing it.**

Depending on the age of your child, you might explain to him that you want to help the teachers learn what he is doing for himself, so that you all can work together to help him become as independent as you know he wants to be. (At least, that is what I did.)

And, if you do want to review concepts, or correct homework, just first be sure to make a copy of what your child did independently. Place that copy in your child binder.

Also, be sure to note whatever help you give that works—whether it's breaking down a problem into parts, or scribing for your child so that he can focus on formulating his ideas. These strategies may be possible modifications for the school to add to your child's IEP.

When should I call a lawyer?

My hope is to empower you to do as much as you can for your children yourself. You are your child's best advocate. And, as a wonderful attorney and friend often says: "None of us have money trees growing in our back yards."

But, there are two occasions when I do believe it is prudent to call a lawyer:

One: **You have done everything right** (in accordance with this book, of course!) and you are still not getting the answers that you are entitled to. In that case, call your local legal aid society or a private attorney for an initial consultation, even if by phone.

Two: You think you are doing everything right, but you would like the peace of mind of a second opinion, and you can afford to buy an hour of an attorney's time for a consult. This might cost you $300, but I consider it an **educational check-up** and consider it very worthwhile (of course, I am an attorney).

Don't forget that you can ask any trusted friend, teacher or provider for their input as well. You never know who will say something that gives you a new thought about your own child's situation. It happens to me when I am speaking with clients all the time.

The behaviorist I hired to work with my son in our home told me that my son is ready to be in an integrated classroom.

When I told the school, the case manager said: "None of the private professionals who see your son have seen him in school, so they can't say what he needs in school."

What do I do?

Bring them in. The law entitles you to observe your child in school. It also allows you to bring your experts, your professionals, in to school to observe. Many parents do not know this.

The law permits this because you are part of the IEP team and the other members of the IEP get to observe your child in school. You need to be able to as well. The school will often limit your observation time—whether of your child in class, or of a program the school wants you to consider. But if the school gives you an outright "no," and won't back down, file for mediation.

My friend has a friend who has a child who needs services but the mom speaks only Spanish. How can I help her?

First, help her to ask the school for a **translator**.

Second, give her a copy of **this book—the Spanish edition**—which is either available right now, or will be available in a matter of weeks.

Note that in New Jersey, and most likely in other states, forms such as the Mediation Request (in the Appendix) are also available in Spanish, free and online. Check the Department of Education website.

You can contact your local legal aid society for the names of organizations that provide services to your local Spanish-speaking community.

Appendix
(including forms and sample letters)

How to Set Up Your Binder for Your Child

This is how I do it:

On the Cover—Place a large, gorgeous picture of your child on front cover

On the Spine—Place on the spine your child's name and the school year—i.e., "Susan Lee, 2017-18 School Year"

Inside front flap—Tuck your copy of this book in the front inside flap

Inside the three rings—

Section One:
Copy of current IEP on top
School schedule
Contact List of teachers, therapists, case manager

Section Two: This section to be arranged *chronologically*, with most recent on top. I include:

·all testing—by school or privately, such as:
> speech evaluations,
> psychological evaluations,
> educational testing,
> medical reports,
> occupational therapy evaluations,
> assistive technology evaluations;

·report cards;

·progress reports (showing progress with respect to IEP goals);

·all communication log pages from calls or meetings with school;

·copies of important emails or other school correspondence;

·examples of school work, tests, handwriting sample;

·last year's IEP and any amendments.

Inside the back flap—lined paper for note-taking.

Bring this binder to every school meeting.

Communication Log Form—
Make copies and keep in the back
pocket of your binder

Date:_____

Time:_____

Location:_____

Person contacted:

Name:_____

Title:_____

Communication—Circle One:

By phone.   In person.   Via mail   Other: _____

What was said:

_____

_____

_____

_____

_____

_____

_____

Action Planned:

_____

_____

_____

Any Follow-up required:

_____

_____

_____

_____

Sample Letter Requesting a Child Study Team Meeting

63 High Road
Anytown, New York 10009
September 2, 2017

Dr. William Samuels
Director of Special Services
Anytown, New York 10009

Dear Director of Special Services:

I am writing to you because I am very concerned about my son, Jose. He has been struggling in school and is becoming increasingly frustrated. I suspect that he has learning issues.

Please arrange for a Child Study Team meeting so that he can be evaluated for special education and related services as soon as possible.

I will make every effort to accommodate your team's schedule. Thank you very much for your caring. Please feel free to call me on my cell phone: (xxx-xxx-xxxx), my home phone (xxx-xxx-xxxx) or to reach me via email (xxxxxxxxxx).

I look forward to working with you.

Very Truly Yours,

[signature]

Rosana Polumbo

Working Checklist to Bring to IEP Meetings—Sample Form

This is a form that I believe I first saw in Pete Wright's wonderful book *From Emotions to Advocacy.* The blank form is on the following page so that you can make copies. On the page after that, I share what one of mine looks like, after I've filled it out during a progress meeting.

IEP Meeting for: _____

Date: _____

What Mom Wants	School's Response	Resolved?

IEP Meeting for: Mike Smith
Date: February 20, 2016

Parent Requests	School's Response	Resolved?
Speech Evaluation	Will do before June; mom asks that evaluator go into unstructured school time to observe use of pragmatic language	Yes
Increase OT to twice a week	No; but will monitor	No; revisit in 8 weeks
Communication Book be written in daily	Will do	Yes
Assistive tech eval.	Not sure necessary	Will revisit in 8 weeks at which point mom may request updated OT eval
ESY (Extended School Year Programming)	Will be considered in May	No; revisit in 8 weeks
IEP to reflect current diagnosis of Autism Spectrum Disorder from outside provider	IEP will be revised to include	Yes; Mom to receive updated IEP and confirm
Mom requests modification of extended time for completion of assignments	Agreed.	Yes.

Sample "Thank You" Follow-up Note to School Team Following an IEP Meeting

76 Spruce Street
Manalapan, Ohio 98786
October 20, 2018
[your email address]

Ms. Vikki Smart
Manalapan Board of Education
Department of Special Services
302 Elm Street
Manalapan, Ohio 98786

Dear [Case Manager]:

Thank you to you and the entire team for meeting with me today about Jack. I appreciate your caring and willingness to work with me to come up with solutions. It is my understanding that you will be adding an extra thirty-minute session of Speech each week as soon as I return to you the IEP Amendment that you gave to me at the meeting.

I also understand that we will be meeting in eight weeks and that at this meeting we will further discuss Jack's handwriting and re-consider my request at today's meeting that the school perform an assistive technologies evaluation for Jack before the end of the school year. Kindly email possible times to me so I can block out that time on my calendar.

Please let me know if you need anything further from me. It is a pleasure to work with this team.

Very Truly Yours,

[your name]

Potential Placements and Programs

I list them here, roughly in order from most restrictive to least. In fact, this determination must be made individually, for each child. The school is required to consider each less restrictive environment, before moving to a more restrictive one.

Home instruction (often for medical reasons, or while an appropriate placement is located. It may occur at home, in a public library, or in school after hours.)

Private specialized school for children with particular special needs

Public out-of-district programs (for instance, if your school does not have the ABA program your child needs, but a public school district nearby does)

Self-contained programs in district:

—"LLD" classes for children with language-based learning disabilities

—"ABA" based programs that use applied behavior analysis (often for children with autism spectrum diagnoses)

—Multiply disabled ("MD") classrooms

—Classrooms for children with emotional or behavioral challenges

Other programs in district:

—*Inclusion Classes.* Classes in-district, in which general education and special education students are educated side-by-side. Classes have two teachers—a general education teacher and a special education teacher—who are both in the classroom. The special education teacher is able to provide extra support for children who have IEPs.

Some children have in-district programs that consist of a child attending a general education class for most of the day, but leaving class to attend a *resource room* (a self-contained, smaller, special education class taught by a special education teacher) for certain classes—often math and/or language arts.

Combination programs. For example, programs consisting of a portion of the day in a self-contained class such as an ABA program, with a portion of the day spent in a general education classroom or another classroom, such as a self-contained LLD classroom. These programs can be a first step towards transitioning to a less restrictive environment for your child.

***

Note that "related services"—such as speech and occupational therapy—can also often be provided as "push in" whereby the therapist goes into the child's class, or "push out" whereby the child works with the therapist (and possibly a few other students) outside the class. Push in services can show the therapist real-time challenges, and reduce disruptions in a child's day.

***

Also note that each school and each school district is not required to have each program in each school. The law does require that if they do not have the program the child needs, the school needs to cast its net wider, until it finds it—or, it needs to create the program the child needs.

Be creative. Don't be afraid to say, "I like this program, except it does not address X. What can we think of together that we can add to meet that need?"

Don't be afraid to say, "What if we used a part of this program, but added a portion of the day in another program?"

Ask to see the programs offered. Your gut will tell you if the environment and peer group is appropriate for your child.

Sample Mediation Request

On the following page, I provide a sample mediation request form. Each state should make its form available on its Department of Education website. Parents do not need an attorney or advocate to file it. Be sure you to send it to the address or addresses listed.

A very recent change is that your Department of Education may now accept forms submitted electronically; just check the directions, usually printed at the beginning of the form.

I have completed this form for a fictitious student, to give you a sense of how it looks when it is completed, and how little you need to include.

Please see the Crucial Questions section for more information about when and how to file for mediation, and about what happens next when you do file.

If you need an interpreter to be present at mediation, write that you need an interpreter at mediation and specify the language you need.

Parental Request for
Mediation/Due Process Hearing/Expedited
Due Process Hearing

PLEASE NOTE: In accordance with IDEA 2004, you must complete all the information requested as fully and accurately as possible. Also, you must identify the specific reasons for the disagreement with the identification, evaluation, eligibility, classification, placement or provision of programs or related services for your child. If the information is incomplete or the reasons for your disagreement are vague or unclear, the district may challenge the sufficiency of your request for a due process hearing. Requests for mediation only are not subject to a sufficiency challenge.

The entire petition must be filed with the Office of Special Education Programs (OSEP) and one copy of the entire petition must be filed with the district.

Beginning July 1, 2016, the (OSEP) will accept requests for mediation, a due process hearing, emergent relief (petition only; attachments must be sent separately via regular mail) electronically through an OSEP-maintained and monitored email address. The newly created email address will be used exclusively for the submission of requests and will not be used to communicate with the parties or their representatives. Completed petitions must be saved as Adobe PDF documents and submitted as an attachment to an email sent to: osepdisputeresolution@doe.state.nj.us. Adobe Acrobat Reader is document reader software that is available for free download at: https://get.adobe.com/reader/. Please note that requests for a complaint investigation, enforcement of a mediation agreement or enforcement of a final decision will NOT be accepted via electronic mail and must be mailed or faxed to the OSEP to be accepted and processed.

*Date: **May 6, 2016**

To: Director
       Office of Special Education Programs
       NJ Department of Education
       P.O. Box 500
       Trenton, NJ 08625-0500

*From: **Jill R. Smith**

      Full name of parent(s) submitting the request

Address:

6 Spruce Street

Orange, New Jersey 07932

*County: **Union**

*Home Phone: **(999) 999-9999**

*Fax: **(999) 999 -9999**

*Work Phone: **(999) 999-9999**

*Cell Phone: **(999) 999-9999**

*Please check whether you will be represented by __an attorney or assisted by __an advocate.

*Name of attorney or advocate: **none**

*Address: _____

*Phone: (____) ____ - _____

---

* Items marked with an asterisk are not required; however, providing the requested information will assist in expediting your request.

*Fax: (_____) _____ - _____

Child's Name: **Bill Smith**   *Date of Birth: **12/2/14**

*Child's Address (If different from parent's address):

_____

_____

_____

*District of Residence (district in which parent resides):

Union

 School the student attends: **The Coop Preschool**

*District where the school is located: **Union**

*Disability category: **The school did not give Bill one.**

Please check **ONE** of the following boxes:

X　　**Mediation Only** - Please complete items 1 through 5 below

___　　**Due Process Hearing** - Please complete items 1 through 5 below

___　　**Expedited Due Process Hearing** _for disciplinary matters only_ - Please complete items 1 through 5 below

****

1. **Required Steps for a Due Process Hearing or an Expedited Due Process Hearing (discipline matters only)** – When a parent requests a hearing, the district is given an opportunity to resolve the matter before

the hearing is scheduled. The district is required to conduct a resolution session (within 15 days for a due process hearing and 7 days for an expedited due process hearing) and you are required to participate. You and the district may choose to participate in mediation conducted by the OSEP in place of a resolution session, or both parties can agree to waive the resolution session and proceed directly to a hearing.

Upon receipt of this notice, a representative of the school district must contact you to arrange a resolution session. If you would like to have the district consider other options, please check <u>ONE</u> of the following:

<u>X</u> I am requesting a mediation conference conducted by the OSEP in place of a resolution session. **If the district agrees to mediation in place of a resolution session, a representative of the district must contact the OSEP at 609-984-1286 to facilitate the scheduling of the mediation conference.**

__ I want to waive the resolution conference and proceed directly to a due process hearing.

By signing below I am waiving the resolution session and mediation. An authorized representative of the district must also agree *in writing* to waive the resolution period.

Signature: *Jill Smith* _____

2. Please provide a description of the nature of the problem and any facts related to the problem. Attach additional sheets as needed:

Bill's doctor diagnosed autism and says that Bill needs an IEP. School said that Bill is not eligible. I disagree.

3. Please provide a description of how this problem could be resolved. Attach additional sheets as needed:

This problem could be resolved by the school's agreeing to classify Bill and working with me to develop appropriate IEP. Attached please find: 1) my doctor's diagnosis and recommendations; 2) all public school testing and reports.

4. A copy of this petition must be provided to the other party. Please check to verify.

X   A copy of this request was sent to the superintendent of the school district:

Name of the superintendent: Ms. Vikki Best

Address:
Orange School District Board of Education
303 Elm Street
Orange, New Jersey, 07932

5. Parent's signature: _Jill Smith_

Note to parent(s) requesting a due process hearing: The IDEA Amendments of 2004 provide that attorneys' fees may be reduced if the parent or parent's attorney unreasonably protracted the final resolution of the controversy or the attorney representing the parent did not provide to the district the appropriate information in the due process request.

Sample List of Possible Accommodations

Children with various disabilities have benefited from the following accommodations which may be incorporated into an IEP or 504 Plan, where appropriate. If you believe that your child needs any of the following, suggest them to the IEP team for consideration. Also feel free to suggest any modifications that you believe will help your child.

For more ideas, check the websites for organizations that bring together parents of children who have disabilities that are similar to your child's. Search the web for articles that discuss accommodations for children with a particular challenge.

And, if you find an accommodation or modification that makes sense for your child, discuss it with your terrific team of advisors. Someone on your team may be able to include in their report a recommendation that such modification is "appropriate." Bring that report to your case manager.

Often used for children with **ADHD** or Attention Deficit Hyperactivity Disorder:

·Extended time on tests and quizzes.
·Repeat and reword directions.
·Allow for alternate testing methods.
·Testing in a separate room
·Allow frequent breaks.
·Allow child to use fidgets or other manipulatives.
·Reduce homework to show mastery of concepts.
·Allow use of assistive technology for homework and tests.
·Allow scribing.
·Provide second set of books for home.
·Provide copies of notes.
·Provide study guides in advance.
·Break work down into smaller pieces.
·Assist with organizer.

·Use multi-sensory approach.
·Check frequently for understanding.

***

Often added for children with **anxiety disorders**:

·No surprise tests or quizzes.
·Allow child to discreetly signal teacher (raise hand or show a pass to teacher) and leave to visit safe person without question.

***

Often added for children with **dyslexia**:

·Do not penalize for spelling where not purpose of assignment.
·Allow use of assistive technology or scribing.

***

Often added for children with **auditory processing disorders**:

·Do not grade for accent in foreign language or for oral language.
·Require all tests, assignments and quizzes to be in writing (not given orally.)

Epilogue

If this book made you laugh or cry at any point, I hope you will read my forthcoming book of personal essays, tentatively entitled *"Parenting: A Manual"* (tongue in check, of course!) so that we can continue to laugh and cry together.

Disclaimer: You know, of course, that this book is not intended to provide legal advice or to address your specific situation, the facts of which I cannot know. Plus, the law is filled with details, and it changes. This book is my attempt to provide the most useful distillation I can of what the law says, so that you can be as effective as possible as an advocate. Please let me know if I can make changes to make it more useful to you, and to other parents like you and me.

Disclaimer of Liability on the part of Children's Specialized Hospital: Children's Specialized Hospital shall in no way be held liable for the content of this book. The financial support of Children's Specialized Hospital in making possible the Spanish edition of this book is not intended as, nor shall it be construed as, endorsement of any specific course of action by any individual or as the provision of advice to any individual or group of individuals, legal or otherwise.

CPSIA information can be obtained
at www.ICGtesting.com
Printed in the USA
LVOW11s0944290517
536165LV00002B/545/P